Rookie

Read-About® Geography

The Missouri River

By Christine Taylor-Butler

Subject Consultant
James D. Harlan, Program Manager and Senior Research Specialist
Department of Geography
University of Missouri, Columbia, Missouri

Reading Consultant
Cecilia Minden-Cupp, PhD
Former Director of the Language and Literacy Program
Harvard Graduate School of Education
Cambridge, Massachusetts

Children's Press®
A Division of Scholastic Inc.
New York   Toronto   London   Auckland   Sydney
Mexico City   New Delhi   Hong Kong
Danbury, Connecticut

Designer: Herman Adler Design
Photo Researcher: Caroline Anderson
The photo on the cover shows the Missouri River in Montana.

Library of Congress Cataloging-in-Publication Data

Taylor-Butler, Christine.
  The Missouri River / by Christine Taylor-Butler; subject consultant,
James D. Harlan; reading consultant, Cecilia Minden.
      p. cm. — (Rookie Read-About Geography)
  Includes index.
  ISBN 0-516-25037-X (lib. bdg.)   0-516-29796-1 (pbk.)
  1. Missouri River—Juvenile literature. 2. Missouri River—Geography—
Juvenile literature. I. Title. II. Series.
  F598.T25 2006
  917.8'02—dc22   2005021634

JE
TAY
7/06
C. 1

CHILDREN'S PRESS, and ROOKIE READ-ABOUT®,
and associated logos are trademarks and/or registered trademarks
of Scholastic Library Publishing. SCHOLASTIC and associated logos
are trademarks and/or registered trademarks of Scholastic Inc.

1 2 3 4 5 6 7 8 9 10 R 15 14 13 12 11 10 09 08 07 06

The Missouri River is
the longest river in the
United States.

Long ago, bodies of ice called glaciers moved across the land. The Missouri River formed along the edge of these glaciers.

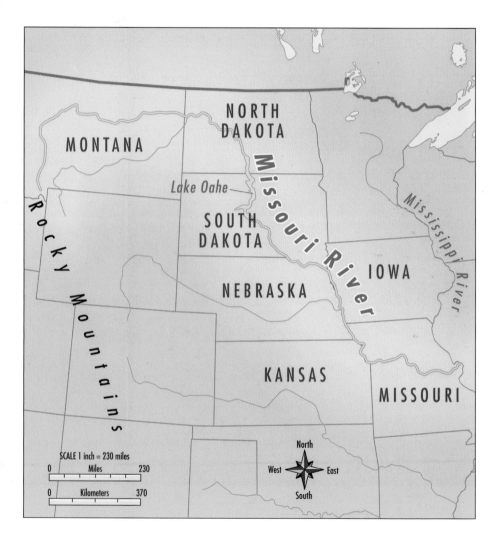

SCALE 1 inch = 230 miles

| 0 | Miles | 230 |

| 0 | Kilometers | 370 |

North
West · East
South

The Missouri River begins in the Rocky Mountains of Montana. It ends in eastern Missouri. It flows through Montana, North Dakota, South Dakota, Iowa, Nebraska, Kansas, and Missouri.

Along the way, many rivers and streams drain into the Missouri River.

The mouth of the Missouri River drains into the Mississippi River. Together, the two form the fourth-longest river on Earth. Only the Amazon, Nile, and Yangtze rivers are longer.

The Missouri River (left) flowing into the
Mississippi River

The Missouri River is
nicknamed Big Muddy.
It appears muddy because
it has a lot of silt in it.

Silt is a mixture of tiny
pieces of sand and rock.

Long ago, people depended
on the river for travel.

Native Americans paddled
through the shallow water
in dugout canoes.

Later, people used
steamboats and barges
to ship goods.

Native Americans in dugout canoes

Explorers Meriwether Lewis and William Clark (right)

Meriwether Lewis and William Clark were famous explorers. They traveled the Missouri River during the early 1800s. They used the river to find a route to the Pacific Ocean.

The Missouri River once had very strong currents.

The river often flooded after a heavy rain. The floods damaged homes, farms, and businesses.

In 1944, a plan was developed to control flooding along the Missouri River.

Six dams were built on the river. These dams calmed the currents. There are fewer floods now.

Dams on the Missouri
River have other jobs,
too. They help irrigate,
or water, crops.

Water from the dams is
used to make electricity.

An irrigation system connected to the Missouri River

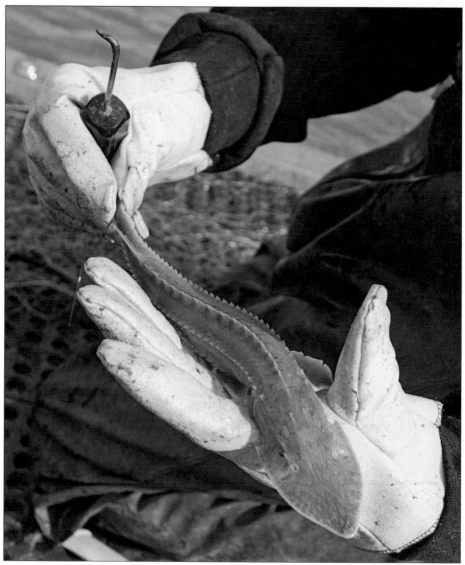

Fish such as this sturgeon live in the Missouri River.

Dams along the Missouri River also create problems. They trap sediment needed to keep the river healthy. Sediment is a mixture of rocks, sand, and dirt. It is carried by wind, water, or glaciers.

The Missouri River is smaller because of dams. This harms plants and animals.

The Missouri River is the biggest reservoir system in North America. Reservoirs are areas used for storing large amounts of water.

Reservoirs such as Lake Oahe have deep water. Fish such as rainbow smelt and chinook salmon live there.

Lake Oahe

People fish and camp along the Missouri River. They boat and watch wildlife.

Would you like to visit the
Missouri River?

What would you do first?

Words You Know

dams

dugout canoes

floods

irrigate

30

Lake Oahe

Mississippi River

Index

About the Author

Christine Taylor-Butler is the author of twenty-one books for children. She is a graduate of the Massachusetts Institute of Technology. She is also the author of two other books in the Rookie Read-About® Geography series: *Missouri* and *Kansas*. Christine lives in Kansas City, Missouri. The Missouri River passes by this area. It *does* flood, and it *is* muddy!

Photo Credits

Photographs © 2006: Airphoto-Jim Wark: 3, 9, 18, 25, 30 top left, 31; AP/Wide World Photos/L.G. Patterson: 22; Corbis Images: 17, 30 bottom left (Najlah Feanny), 5 (David Muench), 10 (Charles E. Rotkin), 14 (Alfred Russell/Bettmann), 29 (Scott T. Smith), 26 (Dale C. Spartas); North Wind Picture Archives: 13, 30 top right; PictureQuest/Comstock Images: 21, 30 bottom right; Superstock, Inc./Kent & Charlene Krone: cover.

Map by Bob Italiano